Maths *Key Stage 1*
Pupil Resource Book

Sean McArdle

Text © Sean McArdle 2002
Original illustrations © Nelson Thornes Ltd 2002

Published in 2002 by:
Nelson Thornes Ltd
Delta Place
27 Bath Road
CHELTENHAM
GL53 7TH
United Kingdom

01 02 03 04 05 / 10 9 8 7 6 5 4 3 2 1

A catalogue record for this book is available from the British Library

ISBN 0 7487 6371 6

Printed and bound in Great Britain by The Bath Press

Nelson Thornes publishes a comprehensive range of teacher resource books in the *Blueprints* and *Learning Targets* series. These titles provide busy teachers with unbeatable curriculum coverage, inspiration and value for money. For a complete list, please call our Primary Customer Services on 01242 267280, send an e-mail to cservices@nelsonthornes.com or write to:

Nelson Thornes Ltd, Freepost, Primary Customer Services, Delta Place, 27 Bath Road, Cheltenham GL53 7ZZ.

All Nelson Thornes titles can be bought by phone using a credit or debit card on 01242 267280 or online by visiting our website – www.nelsonthornes.com

Contents

Contents

Introduction

The photocopiable activity sheets in this book have been designed to complement the materials in the *Blueprints Maths Key Stage* 1: *Teacher's Resource Book*. All of the materials are new and have been written to give teachers good resources which match the needs of the mathematics National Curriculum and the ideas promoted in the National Numeracy Strategy. The mathematics curriculum used in most schools is heavily covered.

It is likely that the activity sheets will mainly be used with infants but are suitable for less able children higher up the school. The requirement for the children to read text has been kept to a bare minimum in the context of both the questions and the explanations. Inevitably, some reading is necessary on some activity sheets. The less able children in Year 2 and many Year 1 children will need some explanation of some of the tasks but this would be expected whatever the work. Correct use of mathematical language is encouraged throughout the series.

It should also be noted that not all the activity sheets include explicit instructions for the children to follow. Such instructions that do appear can only be abbreviated guidelines. Irrespective of any printed instruction, the children will, of course, follow your own instructions and explanations of the activity they are to undertake.

Many of the activity sheets are differentiated in the sense that they contain work of varying difficulty. It is expected that as part of normal good practice, teachers will use the activity sheets in the most appropriate ways to suit their classes.

A small number of activity sheets are not directly related to the National Numeracy Strategy but relate to the inclusion of the number 31 as a developmental point between knowledge of numbers to 20 (Year 1) and 100 (Year 2). This has been done because many teachers find the jump from 20 to 100 to be rather large for some children and a stepping stone is helpful. Thirty-one is sometimes used as this stepping stone because it is often the number in an infant class (including the teacher) and can therefore be used for various counting, addition and subtraction games. It is also the maximum number of days in a month and the children will know the numbers because of important events, especially birthdays and, finally, it crosses the boundary between the twenties numbers which are usually well known and the thirties, the next major step in developing towards 100.

The book also contains more general resources including templates for number and coin fans. Such equipment is becoming widely used and, although tedious to make in the first place, they can be of great benefit to children of all abilities.

The completed activity sheets may be retained as evidence and the final part of the book contains record sheets which should help keep track of the work each child has done.

Each activity sheet in *Blueprints Maths Key Stage* 1: *Pupil Resource Book* is linked to an activity page in *Blueprints Maths Key Stage* 1: *Teacher's Resource Book*. The link is made explicit through the numbers in the hand prints in each book.

Introduction

Activity sheet number in the hand print in the *Pupil Resource Book* also on the relevant page (top left) in the *Teacher's Resource Book*

Linked *Teacher's Resource Book* page number appears in the bottom-right corner of the relevant activity sheet in the *Pupil Resource Book*

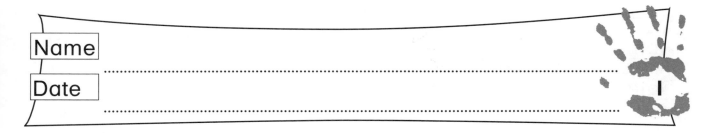

Number names to 20

Join the numbers

	3	five
	9	ten
	5	fifteen
	15	twenty
	11	one
	8	three
	14	six
	4	nine
	12	eighteen
	16	twelve
	20	two
	17	four
	1	eight
	19	fourteen
	7	sixteen
	10	seventeen
	18	seven
	6	eleven
	13	nineteen
	2	thirteen

Blueprints Maths Key Stage 1: Pupil Resource Book © Sean McArdle, Nelson Thornes Ltd, 2002

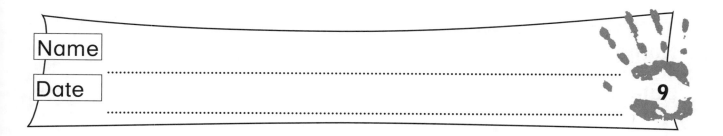

Odds and evens

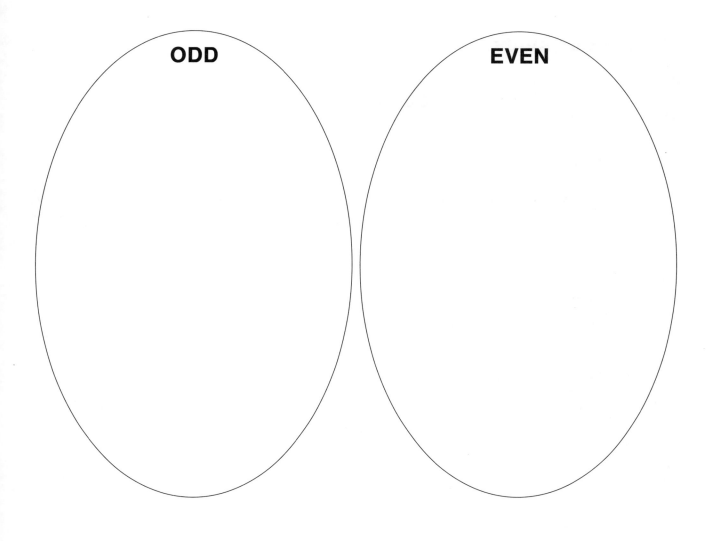

ODD

EVEN

| 1 | 2 | 3 | 4 | 5 | 6 | 7 | 8 |

| 9 | 10 | 11 | 12 | 13 | 14 | 15 | 16 |

| 17 | 18 | 19 | 20 | 21 | 22 | 23 | 24 |

30 39 46 61 77 93

Blueprints Maths Key Stage 1: Pupil Resource Book © Sean McArdle, Nelson Thornes Ltd, 2002

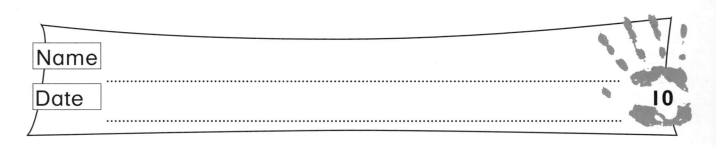

Steps of five and three

Colour our steps

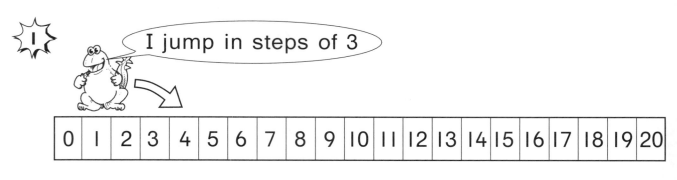

I jump in steps of 3

0	1	2	3	4	5	6	7	8	9	10	11	12	13	14	15	16	17	18	19	20

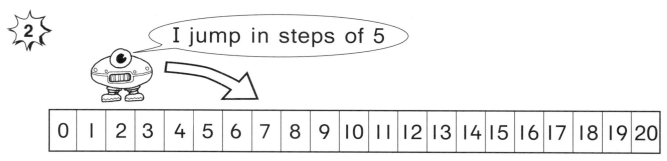

I jump in steps of 5

0	1	2	3	4	5	6	7	8	9	10	11	12	13	14	15	16	17	18	19	20

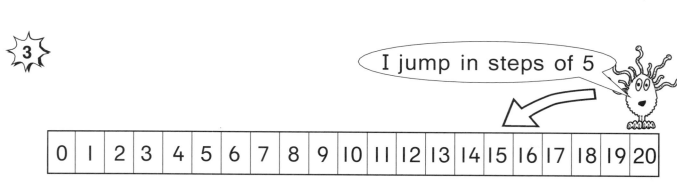

I jump in steps of 5

0	1	2	3	4	5	6	7	8	9	10	11	12	13	14	15	16	17	18	19	20

I jump in steps of 3

0	1	2	3	4	5	6	7	8	9	10	11	12	13	14	15	16	17	18	19	20

Blueprints Maths Key Stage 1: Pupil Resource Book © Sean McArdle, Nelson Thornes Ltd, 2002

Steps of three, four and five

1	2	3	4	5	6	7	8	9	10
11	12	13	14	15	16	17	18	19	20
21	22	23	24	25	26	27	28	29	30
31	32	33	34	35	36	37	38	39	40
41	42	43	44	45	46	47	48	49	50
51	52	53	54	55	56	57	58	59	60
61	62	63	64	65	66	67	68	69	70
71	72	73	74	75	76	77	78	79	80
81	82	83	84	85	86	87	88	89	90
91	92	93	94	95	96	97	98	99	100

1 Five steps forward

2 Four steps forward

3 Five steps backwards

Multiples of 2, 5 and 10

Colour the multiples of 2

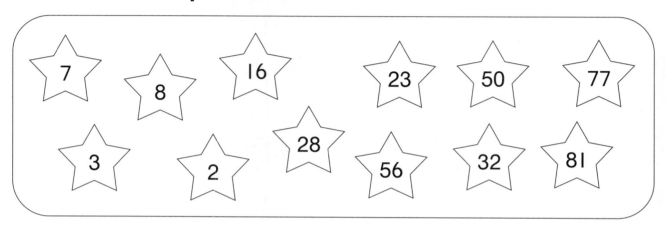

7 8 16 23 50 77

3 2 28 56 32 81

Colour the multiples of 5

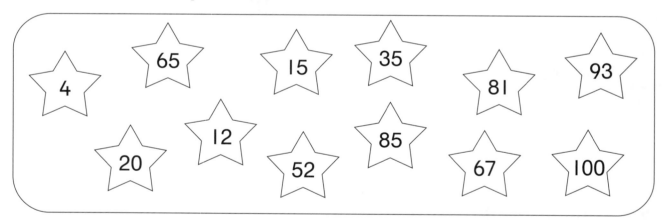

4 65 15 35 81 93

20 12 52 85 67 100

Colour the multiples of 10

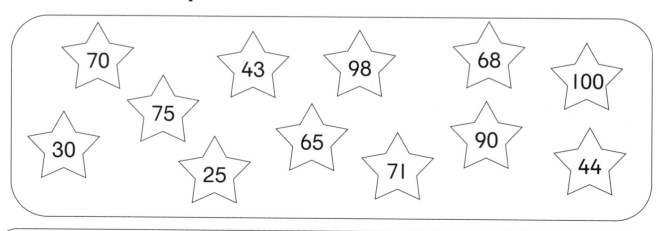

70 43 98 68 100

75 30 25 65 71 90 44

Read and write numbers 20/100

Join the dog to its number.
The first one has been done for you.

Partitioning

Count and partition

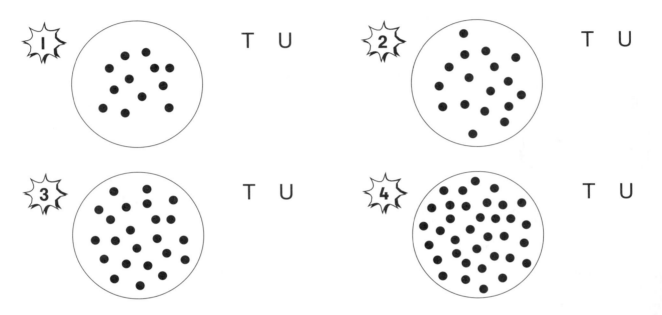

1.   T U

2.   T U

3.   T U

4.   T U

5. **Write the number in the box**

T	U
1	3

T	U
4	0

T	U
6	2

T	U
0	4

T	U
3	5

T	U
0	8

T	U
4	6

T	U
0	5

Blueprints Maths Key Stage 1: Pupil Resource Book © Sean McArdle, Nelson Thornes Ltd, 2002

0 as place holder

1 Write the missing number

$20 + 7 = \boxed{}$

$10 + \boxed{} = 18$

$43 = 3 + \boxed{}$

$81 = 1 + \boxed{}$

$40 + \boxed{} = 46$

$\boxed{} + 9 = 79$

$38 = 30 + \boxed{}$

$60 + \boxed{} = 63$

$60 + 4 = \boxed{}$

$92 = 90 + \boxed{}$

2 Write the missing amount

$20p + 8p = \boxed{}$

$36p = 30p + \boxed{}$

$50p + \boxed{} = 57p$

$80p + 9p = \boxed{}$

$62p = 60p + \boxed{}$

$\boxed{} + 5p = 45p$

Blueprints Maths Key Stage 1: Pupil Resource Book © Sean McArdle, Nelson Thornes Ltd, 2002

Order whole numbers to 100

Set A   **Lower numbers**

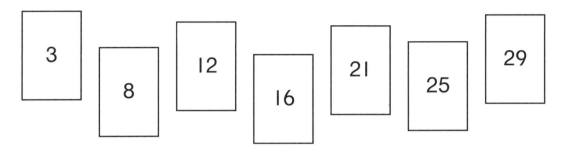

Set B   **Crossing tens boundary set**

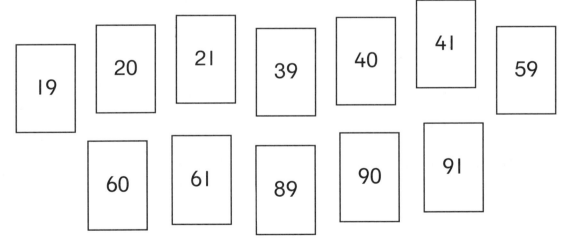

Set C   **Reversal set**

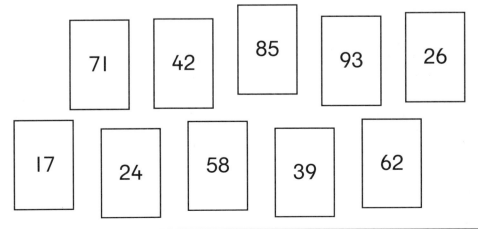

Sensible guesses to 20/50, vocabulary

Estimate – do not count!

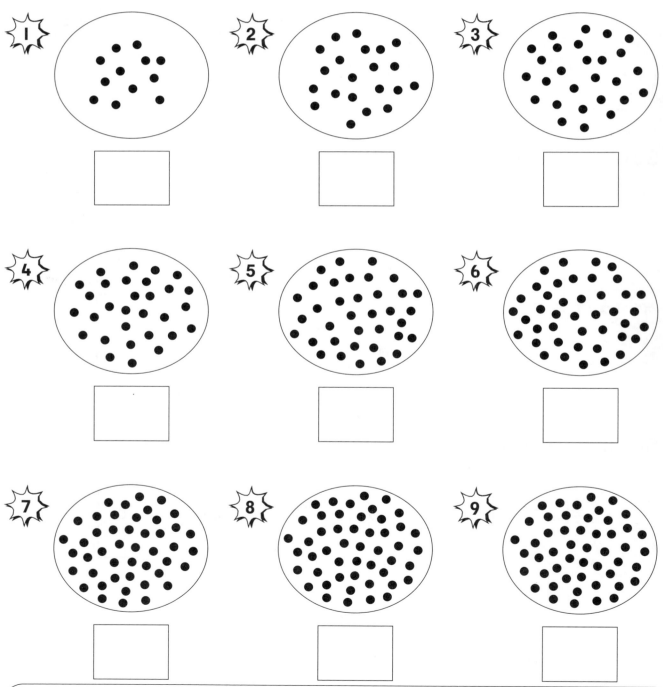

Rounding to nearest ten

Nearest 10p

Half and quarter

Halve and quarter each shape

Equivalence

	Draw ½ of the apples
	Draw 2/4 of the cherries
	Draw 2/2 of the goldfish
	Draw 2/4 of the bananas
	Draw 4/4 of the worms
	Draw 2/4 of the pears

Blueprints Maths Key Stage 1: Pupil Resource Book © Sean McArdle, Nelson Thornes Ltd, 2002

Understanding subtraction

Find *the difference between* the sets

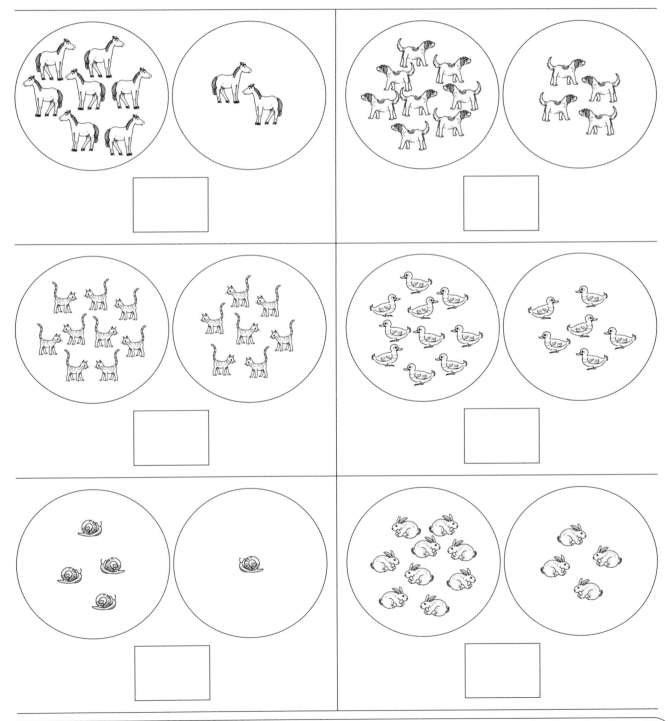

Blueprints Maths Key Stage 1: Pupil Resource Book © Sean McArdle, Nelson Thornes Ltd, 2002

Vocabulary of subtraction

How many are left?

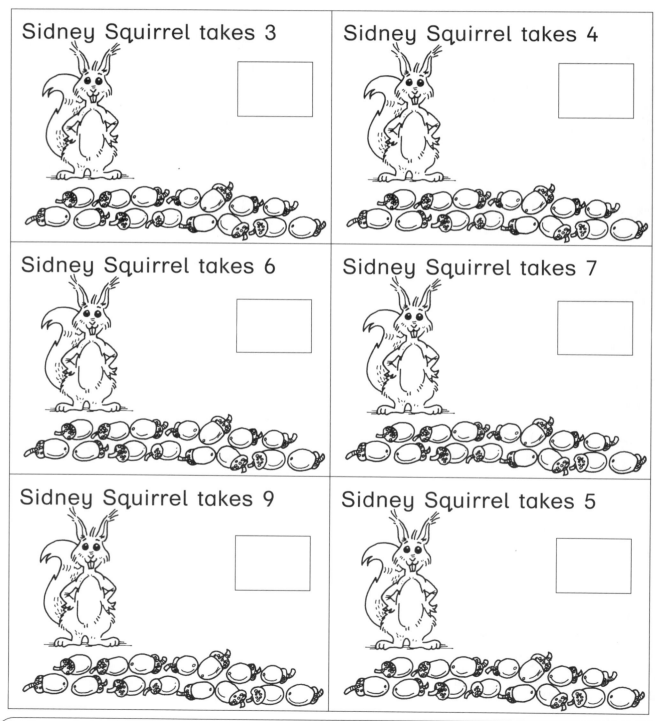

Sidney Squirrel takes 3

Sidney Squirrel takes 4

Sidney Squirrel takes 6

Sidney Squirrel takes 7

Sidney Squirrel takes 9

Sidney Squirrel takes 5

Blueprints Maths Key Stage I: Pupil Resource Book © Sean McArdle, Nelson Thornes Ltd, 2002

The – sign; symbols for unknown numbers

What can I be?

7 take away 3 =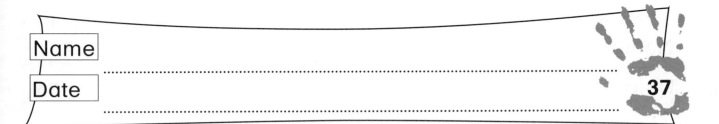

8 take away 2 =

10 take away 4 =

4 take away 4 =

---

10 – 6 =

5 – 5 =

8 – 4 =

12 – 7 =

9 – 2 =

7 – 1 =

---

5 – = 2

8 – = 3

8 – = 1

6 – = 0

7 – = 4

11 – = 5

Recording calculations using symbols

What signs are needed here?

Example

4

+

2

=

6

4

1

3

3

4

7

8

3

11

10

7

3

Addition and subtraction

Teacher's Resource Book page 43

Blueprints Maths Key Stage 1: Pupil Resource Book © Sean McArdle, Nelson Thornes Ltd, 2002

Using symbols in number sentences

Choose the numbers. Write your own numbers to make the sentences true.

☐ − △ = 23   ☆ + ☐ = 12

◯ + △ = 9   ☐ − △ = 15

☐ − ☆ = 8   ☐ − ◯ = 12

☐ − △ = 9   △ − ☐ = 19

△ + ◯ = 30   ☐ + ☆ = 60

☐ − ☆ = 21   ◯ + ☐ = 0

Number bonds to 10 (+ and -)

Put a tick if the sum is correct or a cross if it is wrong

3 + 4 = 7 ✓   3 + 4 = 2 ✗

6 + 1 = 7 ☐   5 − 1 = 4 ☐

9 + 1 = 10 ☐   4 + 2 = 5 ☐

3 + 7 = 10 ☐   7 − 4 = 3 ☐

5 + 5 = 9 ☐   3 − 3 = 0 ☐

8 + 2 = 10 ☐   6 − 4 = 2 ☐

2 + 5 = 7 ☐   10 − 4 = 6 ☐

3 + 6 = 8 ☐   5 + 3 = 8 ☐

10 − 7 = 3 ☐   9 − 5 = 3 ☐

4 + 4 = 8 ☐   7 − 2 = 5 ☐

5 + 4 = 9 ☐   6 + 3 = 10 ☐

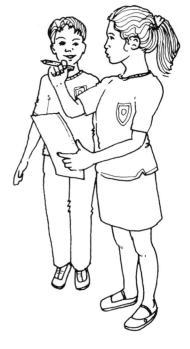

2× and 10× tables

The twos and tens. How long?

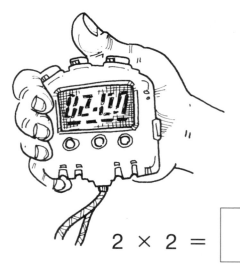

2 × 2 = [ ]   9 × 10 = [ ]

4 × 2 = [ ]   8 × 10 = [ ]

8 × 2 = [ ]   7 × 10 = [ ]

5 × 2 = [ ]   6 × 10 = [ ]

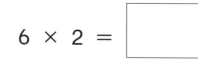

6 × 2 = [ ]   4 × 10 = [ ]

9 × 2 = [ ]   3 × 10 = [ ]

Multiplication facts for 5× table

These cards cost 5p each. How much is each child holding?

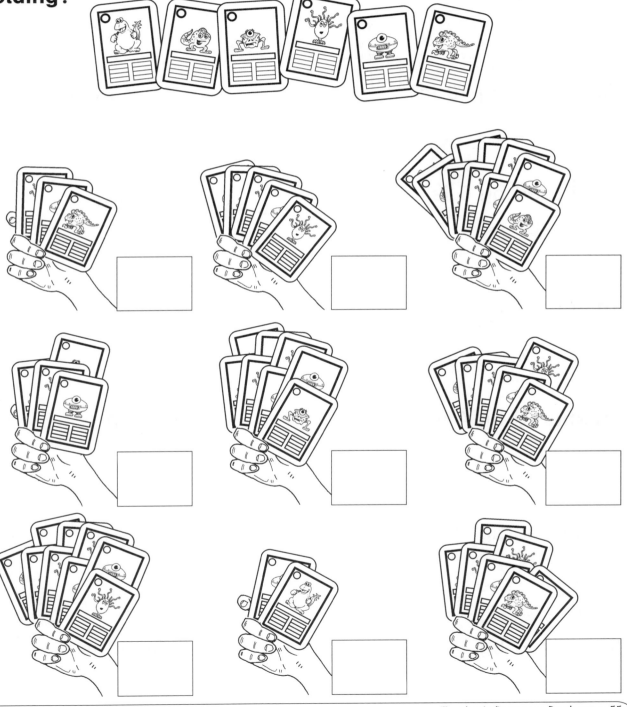

Division, 2×, 10× tables/10-multiples halves

14 shared by 2 is

10 shared by 2 is

50 shared by 10 is

100 shared by 10 is

10 shared by 5 is

16 shared by 2 is

16 shared by 2 is

12 shared by 2 is

40 shared by 4 is

70 shared by 10 is

60 shared by 10 is

18 shared by 2 is

90 shared by 10 is

20 shared by 10 is

Blueprints Maths Key Stage 1: Pupil Resource Book © Sean McArdle, Nelson Thornes Ltd, 2002

Doubles to 15/doubles of multiples of 5

= 5 fingers

 = 6 eggs

= [   ] fingers

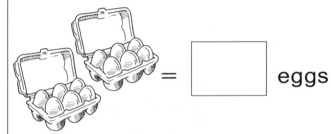 = [   ] eggs

= 7 days

 = 10 pins

 = [   ] days

 = [   ] pins

= 11 players

= 1 year

 = [   ] players

 = [   ] months

Explain in writing and orally

Choose the next shapes

○△○△○△

Why?

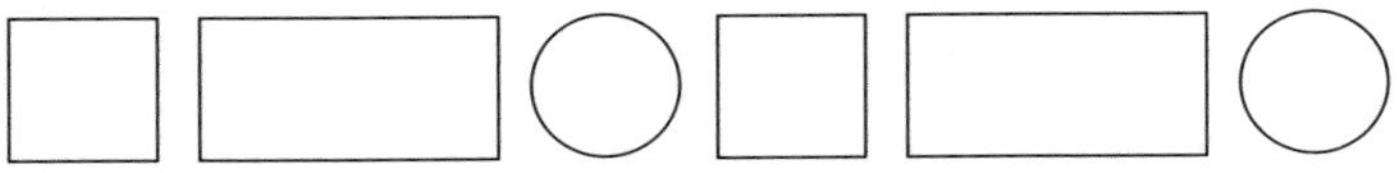

▭▭○○▭○

Why?

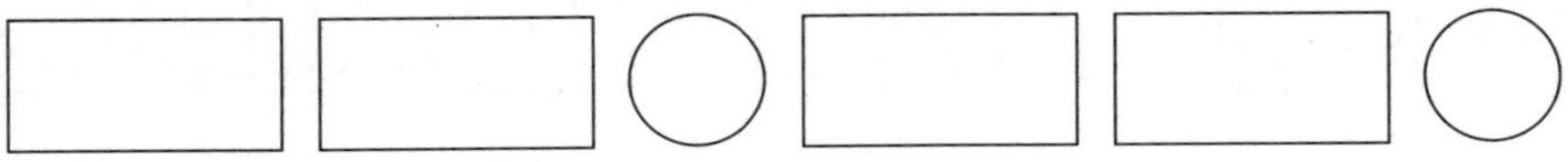

▭▭○▭▭○

Why?

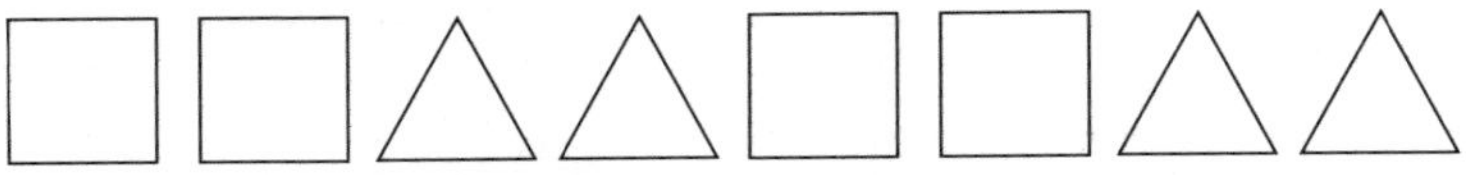

▭▭△△▭▭△△

Why?

Solving 'real life' problems

How many 🍦 each?

Alex   Sandeep

How many animals does

Alex have?

How many animals does

Sandeep have?

How many animals altogether?

How many more with  than ?

Recognise coins of different values

What am I? Fill in the boxes.

Coin colours. List the coins by their colour.

We are copper coloured	We are silver coloured

Find total, give change

How much does the child pay?

Mary buys  **She pays with**

How much change should she have?

Choose which coins

Use as few coins as possible.

Example

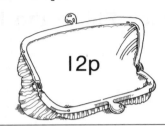

12p

10p	2p

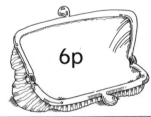

6p

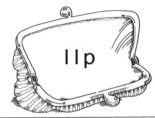

11p

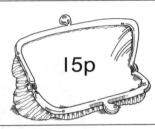

15p

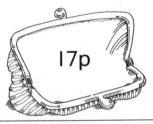

17p

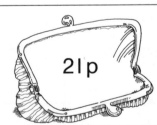

21p

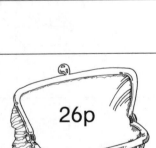

26p

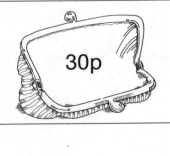

30p

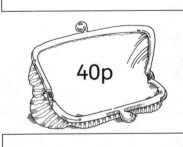

40p

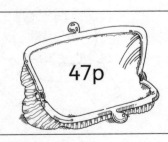

47p

Paying exact sums using small coins

Which coins should you use? Fill in the boxes.

Example

5p	2p	2p

Measure/draw to the nearest centimetre

Measure each line	Draw the line
Length	
Length	
Length	
Length	
Length	
Length	

| Name |
| Date |

Vocabulary of time

What do you do at these times? Write in your answers.

Night	Morning	Afternoon	Evening

Ann   Sol   Aziz

Who is the fastest?

Who is the slowest?

Who is slower than Ug?

Who is faster than Sug?

Use units of time

How many hours?

A maths lesson ☐

In school ☐

Swimming lesson ☐

At lunchtime ☐

Watching TV ☐

How many minutes?

At playtime ☐

Eating breakfast ☐

Reading ☐

Getting dressed ☐

In the bath ☐

Put these in order of length

Day   Second   Hour   Minute   Month

☐

How long it takes

It takes me _____ to _____

It takes me _____ to _____

It takes my teacher _____ to _____

It takes my teacher _____ to _____

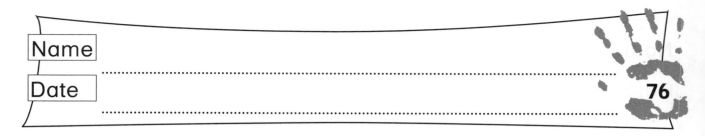

Order events in time

Put these in order please!

Set A

Set B

Set C

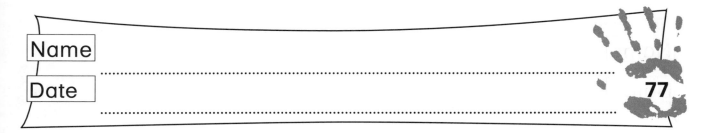

Days of week, seasons, months

Write these in order starting with Monday

Monday   Friday   Tuesday   Saturday
Thursday   Sunday   Wednesday

Monday

Write these in order starting with January

January April October June March September
November February July December August May

January

Join the picture to the season

Spring

Summer

Autumn

Winter

Blueprints Maths Key Stage 1: Pupil Resource Book © Sean McArdle, Nelson Thornes Ltd, 2002

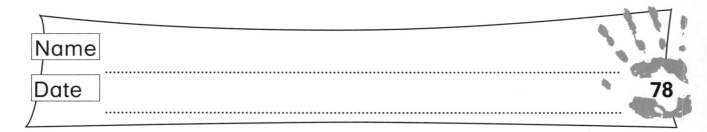

Read time to hour/half-hour (analogue)

What time is it?

Read quarter-hours (analogue)

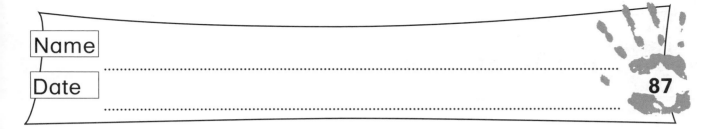

Right angles

Circle the right angles

1–100 number square

1	2	3	4	5	6	7	8	9	10
11	12	13	14	15	16	17	18	19	20
21	22	23	24	25	26	27	28	29	30
31	32	33	34	35	36	37	38	39	40
41	42	43	44	45	46	47	48	49	50
51	52	53	54	55	56	57	58	59	60
61	62	63	64	65	66	67	68	69	70
71	72	73	74	75	76	77	78	79	80
81	82	83	84	85	86	87	88	89	90
91	92	93	94	95	96	97	98	99	100

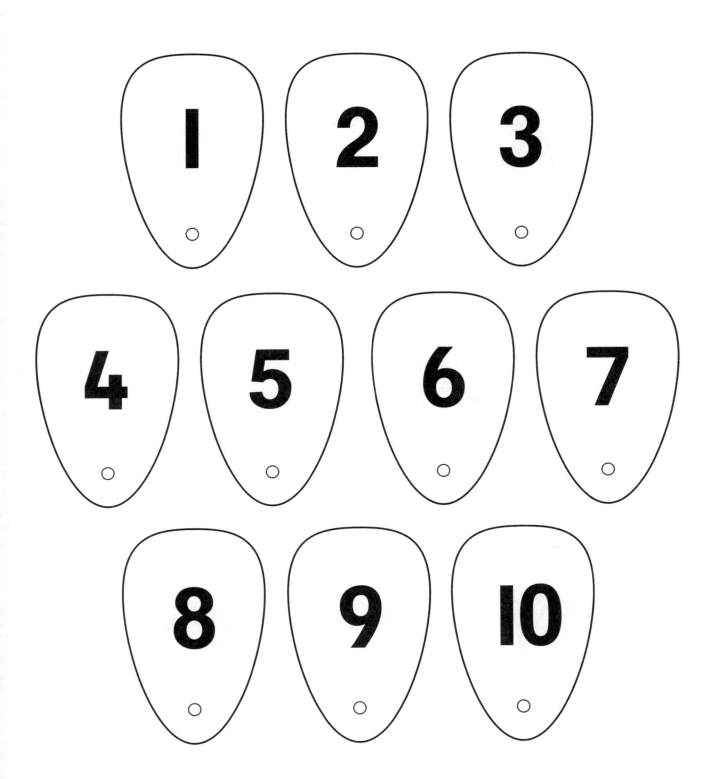

Coin fan templates

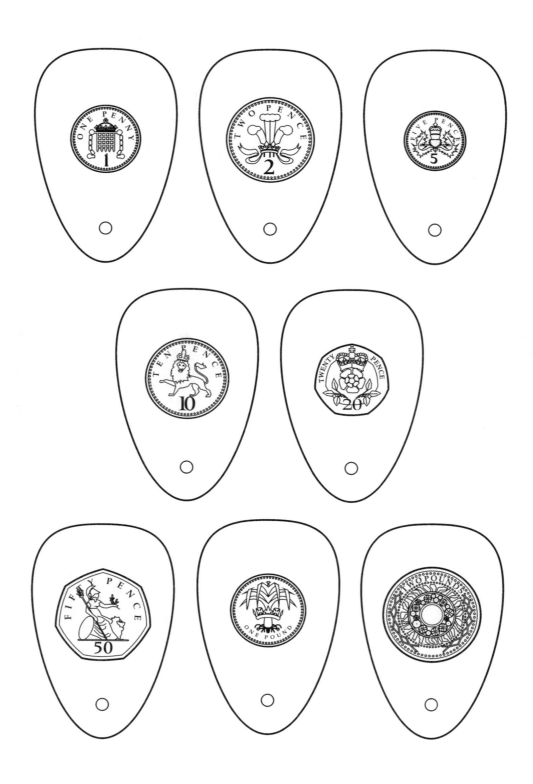

1 cm squares

Record sheet (class teacher)

Child's name	Number names to 20	Number names to 31	Number names to 100	Counting to 20/31	Counting to 100	Counting in ones/tens and hundreds	Counting from any two-digit number	Counting in twos	Odds and evens	Steps of five and three	Steps of three, four and five	Multiples of 2, 5 and 10	Read and write numbers 20/100	Partitioning	0 as place holder

Record sheet (class teacher)

Child's name	Reinforcing activities	Comparing and ordering	Ordinal numbers	More than, less than, between	The = sign and comparing	One more or less	Ten or hundred more or less	Order whole numbers to 100	Sensible guesses to 20/50, vocabulary	Rounding to nearest ten	Half and quarter	Equivalence	Understanding addition	Addition in any order	Using the + sign

Record sheet (class teacher)

Child's name	Number sentences	Symbols for unknown numbers	Adding two or more numbers	Adding three two-digit numbers	Understanding subtraction	Vocabulary of subtraction	The – sign; symbols for unknown numbers	Recording calculations using symbols	Using symbols in number sentences	Addition/subtraction as inverse operations	Addition in different order	Checking	Number pairs totalling ten/bond bingo	Multiples of 10 totalling 100	Addition doubles and halves to 10